MEETING
[GOD]
in
Scripture

Understanding

SPIRITUAL GIFTS

Other titles in the series

MEETING
[GOD]
in
Scripture

Continue exploring the Bible with these spiritual-formation resources.

Entering the Old Testament
Participant's Workbook • 978-0-8358-9945-1 • $10.00
Leader's Guide 978-0-8358-9946-8 • $15.00

Entering the Psalms
Participant's Workbook • 978-0-8358-9973-4 • $10.00
Leader's Guide • 978-0-8358-9975-8 • $15.00

Entering the New Testament
Participant's Workbook • 978-0-8358-9967-3 • $10.00
Leader's Guide • 978-0-8358-9968-0 • $15.00

Order at your local bookstore, by phone, or online.

1-800-972-0433

UpperRoom.org/bookstore

MEETING
[GOD]
in
Scripture

Understanding

SPIRITUAL GIFTS

LEADER'S
GUIDE

MARY LOU REDDING

UPPER
ROOM BOOKS®
NASHVILLE

Cover design: Anderson Design Group
Cover photos: © Shutterstock Images LLC, iStock International Inc., Photos.com
First printing: 2010

ISBN 978-0-8358-1014-2

Printed in the United States of America

Contents

Introduction

*W*elcome to *Meeting God in Scripture: Understanding Spiritual Gifts.* During the next seven weeks, you and your small group will explore spiritual gifts using selected passages from the Bible. *Understanding Spiritual Gifts* is not intended as an exhaustive study of all that the Bible says about spiritual gifts. Rather, it takes a personal, reflective approach, going beyond lists. In addition to completing a self-scored gifts inventory, participants will reflect on their interests, preferences, and talents. As participants read and respond to scripture and participate in small-group sessions, they will be guided to consider prayerfully how God is calling them to use their gifts day by day.

This particular subject of study requires that as the leader of the group, you will have a special role to play by giving attention to those gifts you see in participants. Many people have difficulty seeing themselves as gifted, and so they may need help to claim their gifts and see possibilities for using them. Each week, note abilities, interests, and passions you see in participants as you watch and hear them talk. What makes each one's eyes light up? What does one person or another talk about excitedly? Who sees needs and immediately acts to respond? Who has a gift for listening to others or offering comfort? Who prefers doing rather than "just talk"? (These people may actually use phrases like "put your money where your mouth is" or "where the rubber meets the road.") You may want to prepare a sheet for each person in the group and add observations as the weeks pass. After each session, plan to take a few minutes to record what you notice. In later sessions, these observations will enable you to personalize discussions of gifts and how they are used in ordinary situations.

The daily Bible readings and responses require ten to fifteen minutes a day, and they lead up to and become the starting point for a weekly small-group meeting. Group members who want to do more are encouraged to keep a personal journal; the participant workbook says more about this on pages 8–9.

This leader's guide includes a process and resources for an introductory meeting and six weekly meetings of either 45 or 90 minutes. The time for the introductory meeting may vary, depending on how many persons attend and how long you spend on community-building activities. Using the 45-minute pattern may require you to adjust times for the opening and closing exercises; you will also eliminate the weekly *lectio divina* portion of each session.

In the introductory meeting, you will introduce the approach, process, and content of the remaining sessions. (If your group has completed the sessions in a previous *Meeting God in Scripture* series, the introductory session need not be repeated.) The group will also establish its ground rules. A major goal of this initial gathering is introducing the spiritual-formation approach to reading scripture that makes this experience different than other studies (more about that below).

There are suggestions for how much time to spend on each of the elements of each session noted in this leader's guide. If you try to complete the discussion and reflection activities as a whole group rather than in smaller groups of three or four, you will not be able to complete the activities in the time suggested.

The most important difference between this study and traditional Bible studies is the spiritual-formation approach. To many participants, this approach may seem a dramatic departure from the analytical, left-brain patterns that often characterize Bible study. The preparatory meeting will acquaint participants with the difference between "formational" and "informational" reading of the Bible.

Meeting Format

The first 90-minute session includes get-acquainted activities and a group-exploration of a scripture passage (Exploring the Word). Each session (after the introductory session) includes these components:

- Opening
- Interacting with the Word (in triads)
- Exploring the Word (group activity)
- Engaging the Word (*lectio divina* for 90-minute format only)
- Closing

Detailed directions for leading *lectio divina* appear following this introduction. Charts and descriptions included in this leader's guide may be used to create handouts and/or a computer presentation. Reading the article "What Is Spiritual Formation?" (pages 59–64) will ready you for the introductory session's exploration activity. The additional articles will give you valuable background for leading this study: "Moving Forward in Spiritual Formation," "Meeting God in Service," "Meeting God in Community," and "Meeting God in Everyday Life."

Preparing the Meeting Space

The activities in this study aim to involve participants on sensory and affective levels; you will also want to create a sense of holy space in your meeting location in which to listen to God. With these aims in mind, create a worship center in the meeting space. This may be a simple arrangement on a small table with a Christ candle, a cross, and a few other Christian symbols. Or you may decorate the table with draped cloth and liturgical elements that change weekly. Perhaps someone in the group has special gifts for this and would enjoy taking responsibility for preparing the worship center each week.

Each session will include conversation in twos or threes about the week's Bible readings and the responses, so arrange chairs to allow participants to face one another or in a way that can be easily reconfigured. Tables in the room can provide a surface for group members to write and do activities.

When sessions include handouts, distribute these before participants arrive to save time, reduce confusion, and create a more peaceful atmosphere. If you plan to use a projection system for transparencies or a computer presentation, check these out before each session to reduce technological problems and save time.

Looking Ahead: Supplies/Special Arrangements

All sessions: Always have on hand newsprint or whiteboard and markers, extra Bibles, hymnals and/or means to provide music, worship-center materials

Intro session: Participant's workbooks for all members; modeling clay or Play-Doh for each participant; photocopies of "Obstacles to Hearing God in Scripture" (page 11) and "Informational and Formational Reading" (page 14) for each participant. For the alternate activity: large sheets of paper, pencils, markers.

Session 1: Large pieces of newsprint, one for each group of two persons, the list of questions in Interacting with the Word (page 24).

Session 2: Participant's workbooks (for Spiritual Gifts Inventory Statements and score sheet), the list of questions in Interacting with the Word (page 28), newsprint or computer projection of closing body prayer.

Session 3: Participant's workbooks (for Spiritual Gifts Key and Definitions); photocopies of Spiritual Gifts Clusters and Scripture Translations to hand out (see pages 54–58); the list of questions in Interacting with the Word (page 32); poster or computer presentation of Buechner quotation in Exploring the Word.

Session 4: The list of questions in Interacting with the Word (page 36); large sheets of paper for maps in Exploring the Word, pens, pencils, markers.

Session 5: A ball of multicolored yarn, the list of questions in Interacting with the Word (page 40), copies of the questions under Exploring the Word.

Session 6: A small, empty, gift-wrapped box for each participant (the boxes should be about the same size but wrapped differently with a gift tag on each; put a participant's name in the *To* space, and *God* in the *From* spot), the list of questions in Interacting with the Word (page 44).

Obstacles to Hearing God in Scripture

Common obstacles:

- thinking/talking about scripture

- classifying

- comparing

- describing

- explaining

- looking for "the lesson" rather than listening to scripture:

  the actual words that are there

  the emotions we feel

  the connections we make

  the memories that arise

The Process for Group *Lectio Divina*

STEP ONE: (first-stage reading) Tell group members that you will read the passage twice, once to orient them to its overall content and then again, more slowly, so that they can listen for a word or phrase that stops them or gets their attention. Read the passage aloud, twice.

In the silence, repeat your word or phrase to yourself and reflect on it.

Allow three minutes of silence for reflection.

STEP TWO: **Within your group, repeat the word or phrase that attracted you—without comment, summary, or analysis. (Or you may pass.)**

STEP THREE: (second-stage reading) Ask group members to listen as you read the passage again, slowly, being open to how it connects to them. (Tell them that their word or phrase may or may not be the same one on this reading as during the first reading.)

In silence, consider how your word or phrase connects to your life right now—a situation, a feeling, a possibility.

Allow three minutes of silence for reflection.

STEP FOUR: (At this point, tell the group that participants may always choose not to speak by saying "pass" when their turn comes.)

In your groups, take a few minutes each to tell about the connection you sense between your life and your word or phrase. (Or you may pass.)

Ask the person closest to you in each group to be the first speaker.

STEP FIVE: (third-stage reading) Ask the alternate reader to read the passage again, slowly. Invite group members to listen during this reading for an invitation from God for the next few days:

In the silence, consider what invitation you hear from God. Be open to a sensory impression, an image, a song, a fragrance.

Allow three minutes of silence for reflection.

STEP SIX: Ask group members to ponder in silence the invitation they heard. Allow several minutes of silence.

STEP SEVEN: Invite each person to speak about the invitation he or she senses from God for his or her life in the next few days:

In your groups, allow each person to tell about the invitation he or she heard. (Or you may pass.)

This time, have the person farthest from you to begin. This is an important step in the process, so allow ample time for each person to speak. Watch the groups; check to see which are finishing up, which need more time. Do not rush the process.

STEP EIGHT: Invite persons to pray for each other, one by one in turn, within their smaller groups. Ask each one to pray for the person to his or her right. The group members can decide whether they will pray aloud or silently.

Pray for each other to be empowered to respond to the invitations you heard. (You may pray silently or aloud.)

Remind participants to remain silent when their group finishes praying, since other groups may still be in prayer. When all have finished praying, say "amen" to end the process.

You may want to debrief this experience of *lectio divina* by asking the group as a whole to comment on it: What worked for them? What was difficult about this way of responding to scripture? Have they been led through this process before, and, if so, what was different, better, or worse about it this time? This would be a good time to mention that everyone responds differently to the various ways of exploring scripture and that there is no expected outcome.

Informational and Formational Reading

Reading for information is an integral part of teaching and learning. But reading is also concerned with listening for the special guidance, for the particular insight, for your relationship with God. What matters is the attitude of mind and heart.

Informational Reading

1. Informational reading is concerned with covering as much material as possible and as quickly as possible.

2. Informational reading is linear— seeking an objective meaning, truth, or principle to apply.

3. Informational reading seeks to master the text.

4. In informational reading, the text is an object out there for us to control.

5. Informational reading is analytical, critical, and judgmental.

6. Informational reading is concerned with problem solving.

Formational Reading

1. Formational reading is concerned with small portions of content rather than quantity.

2. Formational reading focuses on depth and seeks multiple layers of meaning in a single passage.

3. Formational reading allows the text to master the student.

4. Formational reading sees the student as the object to be shaped by the text.

5. Formational reading requires a humble, detached, willing, loving approach.

6. Formational reading is open to mystery. Students come to the scripture to stand before the Mystery called God and to let the Mystery address them.

Adapted from *Shaped by the Word: The Power of Scripture in Spiritual Formation*, rev. ed., by M. Robert Mulholland Jr. (Nashville, TN: Upper Room Books, 2000), 49–63. Used by permission.

Permission is granted to make one copy for each participant.

Shaped by God

Preparing for the introductory session: Read the article "What Is Spiritual Formation?" (page 59) and the article "Reading Scripture Devotionally" in the participant's workbook (page 11). Look over the chart comparing informational and formational approaches to reading scripture (page 14). Make copies of this chart to give to group members. If you plan to lead *lectio divina* in each session, be sure to provide copies of "Obstacles to Hearing God in Scripture" (page 11).

Note ideas from articles that you feel are important. Review the plan for the introductory session until you feel comfortable leading it, especially the reading from Genesis and the reflection on it. You will need to tailor this session to fit your time frame. An alternate approach to "Exploring the Word" is provided. Other places to save time might include passing out materials without a great deal of discussion.

As people arrive, distribute participant workbooks and invite group members to browse through them.

Opening Prayer (5 minutes)

Light the Christ candle, saying something like: **Each week we will light a Christ candle to welcome Christ into our conversation. It will remain lighted during the sessions as a** reminder that we are engaged in holy conversation as we meet here. Let's pray. (Read the following prayer or another, or pray spontaneously, as you wish.)

Holy and loving God, thank you for your good gifts that fill the world and fill our lives. Be with us in these sessions as we reflect on what you will say to us about our spiritual gifts. Help us to become more faithful disciples because of what we do here. Amen.

Community Building (20 minutes)

Welcome everyone to the study and tell participants this session will allow them time to get to know one another a bit better and receive more information about what to expect during the coming weeks.

Introductions: Invite group members to pair off by finding a person they do not know or the one they know least well in the group. Tell them that after conversation they are going to introduce each other to the group. Give them six minutes to get to know one another (signal when three minutes has passed to be sure the second person has time to speak). Suggest nonthreatening questions to ask, such as how they came to the church they attend, where they live and have lived, where they went to school, what denomination (if any) they grew up in. *Direct them to ask one particular question:* what is your idea of a perfect Saturday afternoon? After six minutes, invite the pairs to introduce each another to the rest of the group, based on their conversation, including a description of his or her perfect Saturday afternoon. Give them one or two minutes each to introduce their conversation partner, depending on the size of the group.

Alternate Introductions for 45-minute session (10 minutes): Have persons introduce themselves. Give people one minute to say whatever they want about themselves, including what they like to do in their leisure time. (If your group is large, you may need to limit this to 30 seconds per person.)

Establishing a Group Agreement (10 minutes)

Most small groups operate with an agreement that includes points such as:

Presence: Attend each meeting unless serious reasons keep you away.

Prayer: Between meeting times, group members pray for one another and for the group's activities together.

Preparation: Group members make the daily readings and exercise a priority, doing them as diligently as life allows.

Participation: Group members will participate honestly and openly in the activities of the sessions.

Confidentiality: What is said within the group remains in the group. Members will not discuss outside the group anything others say within the group.

Courtesy: Group members will listen to one another with respect and without interrupting or engaging in side conversations. When opinions differ, participants will not attempt to persuade others but will listen for what God may be saying in the differences.

Post the words *presence, prayer, preparation, participation, confidentiality,* and *courtesy* on news-print or a board. Mention what each means for this group and ask if folks want to add to or modify these guidelines. You may want to display reminders of your group's agreement in the meeting room each time you gather.

Introducing the Study (20 minutes)

Distribute the participant's workbooks to any who did not receive them as they arrived.

Explain that this study of the Bible probably will be different than other studies partici-pants may have been a part of. There will be no memorizing or outlining. Have partici-pants open their books to page 49 to the entry point related to session 4, day 3. Give them time to read the suggested guided response to Psalm 40:1-3. Ask: **Based on looking at this activity, how does this way of studying the Bible compare to other studies you have done?** List the responses on newsprint.

Next, direct the attention of the group to the article "Reading Scripture Devotionally" (pages 11–14 in participant's workbook). Give people time to read the article. After five minutes, check to see if everyone is finished and allow more time as necessary. When they have completed the reading, ask participants to compare the article's ideas to their responses listed on the newsprint. Where do their ideas echo the article? Where do their ideas differ from those in the article? Ask if the article raised questions or concerns for them and respond to questions. If you don't have an answer to someone's concern, invite the group to respond.

45-minute format (10 minutes): Direct participants to the article and mention pivotal ideas. Ask them to read the article before beginning their daily Bible readings.

Explain that the ideas in the article shape this study. This is not an exhaustive study of all the verses in scripture that mention spiritual gifts. Each day participants will read a short portion of scripture. Then they will read it again and look closely at one verse or a few verses from the passage. They will respond to the day's reading by following the process suggested in each entry point. Each day's reading and activity will take only ten to fifteen minutes to complete.

The starred entry points: In sessions 1 and 3–6, two stars appear alongside the title of one of the five entry points. Direct people to page 23—session 1, day 1—to see a starred entry point. Ask group members to do the starred activity each week even if they are too pressed for time to do them all, because this starred activity will be part of the weekly group meeting. Session 2 has no starred entry point because completing the gifts inventory is the Exploring the Word activity.

Direct attention to the section of the introduction in the participant's workbook titled "If You Want to Do More" (page 8) and talk about keeping a journal. Ask if anyone in the group has kept a journal. If so, ask these persons to tell the group what they got out of the practice. Invite those who journal to bring their journals to the group meetings to record insights and to refer to as a reminder of the week's activities. Emphasize that journal entries and whatever they write in their participant's workbooks are private; no one will ever have to reveal anything he or she has written.

Exploring the Word (15 minutes)

This activity builds on Genesis 2.

Distribute the modeling clay or Play-Doh. Encourage group members to begin manipulating the clay.

Explain that you are going to read some passages from Genesis aloud; you want them to work the clay as they listen. Ask participants to notice the temperature of the clay, its pliability, its weight, and then to begin to knead it, gently and firmly. Then ask them to think of a shape and to begin to form the clay into that shape while you read.

Read aloud Genesis 1:1-31 and 2:1-8. Read Genesis 2:1-8 a second time, more slowly. When you finish reading, allow folks several minutes to finish their clay creations. Then direct them to the entry point for Genesis 2:7 in their participant's workbook (page 20). Ask them to take two minutes to write responses as suggested in the entry point.

Invite group members to talk about what they think the term *spiritual formation* means, in light of working with the clay. Remind them that the Bible readings and entry-point activities in this study are meant to be spiritual-formation opportunities, encouraging them to attend to how God is and has been at work in their lives, helping them become conformed to the image of Christ.

Alternate Activity for Exploring the Word: If *all* members of the group have already done the modeling-clay activity, you may choose to do the following activity instead. You will need large sheets of paper for all participants and various pencils and markers.

Explain that you are going to read some passages from the Bible and then ask reflection questions. Read Ruth 1:6-17. Then read again Ruth 1:8 and 1:16.

Ask group members to ponder in silence relationships that have changed them. After two minutes, invite them to look back over their lives and identify three or four events that made a difference in the individual each has become.

Invite each person to draw a faith-formation tree that incorporates these relationships and events. Guide them with these or similar instructions: **Begin by drawing a line to represent the ground and sketch a tree that includes trunk and branches above the line and roots below. Write or draw on the tree portion above the ground relationships and events known or verifiable by others (essentially, public knowledge) that have formed you. Below the ground line name or draw influences that are not obvious to others but have influenced your development—for example: the faith traditions (or absence of these) in earlier generations of your family, being part of a small group, participating in mission trips, reading/studying particular books and authors, or growing up in a small town or in another country.** Allow five or six minutes for the drawing and writing. Then invite participants to talk with one other person in the group about their trees, allowing two minutes per person. (Indicate when two minutes has passed so both people have a chance to be heard.) Return to the activity above: invite group members to talk about what they think the term *spiritual formation* means, in light of drawing the faith-formation tree.

Discussion: Formational versus Informational Reading (15 minutes)

Distribute copies of the chart comparing the two ways of reading the Bible (page 14). Talk about the entries on the chart and lead group members to compare the two approaches. Point out that our educational system concentrates primarily on developing left-brain, analytical skills in students. Education typically is presented as a linear process focusing on cognitive abilities. To illustrate, ask participants to consider the different attitudes about art classes and math classes in an average school or to think about the constant quantification (grades, reports, assessments) instead of attention to relationships as we educate.

Closing (5 minutes)

First, ask if anyone would like to volunteer to create or arrange the worship center for the sessions. Then ask if someone would like to choose and lead music at the beginning and end of sessions.

Standing in a circle, invite group members to be silent and to think about two people or events that have shaped their faith. After two minutes, ask them to consider the question *What gift did you find in these people or events?* After a minute of silence, invite any who wish to name the gifts, saying, **You do not need to name the person or event—just mention the gift.** Close with a prayer of your own or this one:

Creating God, you have been at work in the world and in us since before we knew you. Thank you for all the gifts you have given to us through those who have loved us and taught us. Thank you for the experiences and the people—even the difficult ones—that have shaped us and made us who we are today. In the coming weeks, give us open ears and open hearts. Help us to respond to your invitation to use our gifts more fully for the good of your people and your world. I pray in the name of Christ, your greatest gift to us. Amen.

Extinguish the candle and say, **Let us go in peace to serve God and our neighbors in all that we do.**

Preparing for Session 1

- Do the daily readings and entry-point activities in the participant's workbook.

- Review the Exploring the Word activity until you feel ready to lead it.

- Review the pattern for leading *lectio divina* and photocopy and/or mark the week's passage for the alternate reader.

- Prepare materials for the worship center, or remind the person who volunteered for this responsibility.

- Choose an appropriate song to sing at opening and closing of session, or remind the volunteer to do this.

- Assemble materials: large pieces of newsprint (one for each group of two persons), the list of questions in Interacting with the Word (page 24).

To Equip

the Saints

NOTE: All meeting outlines are for 90-minute sessions; if you are using this study in a 45-minute session, you will need to omit the *lectio divina* experience.

Opening (5 minutes)

Light the Christ candle and remind the group that Christ is a part of your conversation. Welcome participants back (or welcome new people who did not make it to the introductory session) and review the group agreement: Presence, Participation, Preparation, Prayer, Confidentiality, and Courtesy.

Invite the music leader to lead a song. Then pray this prayer or one of your own:

Holy Spirit, as you filled and changed the disciples at Pentecost, fill us. May your power activate in us the gifts we have been given, that the world may be filled with the radiance of God shining through us. Be with us during this meeting time. May all we do deepen our commitment to serving Christ and those around us. Amen.

Interacting with the Word (15 minutes)

Invite group members to sit in groups of two or three persons. Give them a couple minutes to review their responses to the week's scripture experiences.

Below are several questions the smaller groups (triads) might use when discussing each session's Bible reading and responses. Choose two of the questions—and others you may choose to add—for the discussion this week and gauge the group's response to them. You may use the same questions each week or vary them. Write the questions you'll be using on a board or flip chart.

Encourage group members to listen for God in each person's words. Remind everyone to allow each group member time to respond to a question before the group moves on to the next.

- What scripture passage from the past session do you remember as especially meaningful, and why?
- Which daily exercise did you most enjoy, and which was the most difficult for you?
- How did the daily readings connect to what has been going on in your life this week? Was one especially appropriate? If so, in what way?
- Which exercise surprised you or helped you realize something about yourself?
- How did the daily readings cause you to change some behavior?
- What do you want to remember from this week's readings, and why?

Exploring the Word (20 minutes)

This activity builds on the entry point for 1 Corinthians 12:1, 4-27.

Direct participants to work in pairs. Distribute large pieces of newsprint (one for each group of two persons) and colored markers/pencils/pens. Invite each group of two to read aloud 1 Corinthians 12:1, 4-27 and consider the comparison between the various roles of human body parts and the different gifts, tasks, and roles within the church.

Direct participants to draw an outline of a person on the paper and label it to indicate the possible tasks or contributions each part of the body might represent. What different tasks or roles might each part of the human body suggest? (For example, what resources does a head offer? What might hands represent? the shoulders? the heart? And so on.)

Encourage people to be creative and think specifically, naming as many possibilities as they can. After ten minutes, ask each duo to post its diagram or drawing. Invite everyone to circulate among the presentations to read and admire one another's work. Call the group back together and invite comments.

Engaging the Word (lectio divina, 45 minutes)

Ask for a volunteer to read on the third hearing and direct participants to sit in groups of three.

Use the steps outlined for leading group *lectio* to guide the group through contemplation of **Colossians 3:12-17**.

After *lectio divina*, ask for one or two minutes of silence to allow those who wish to make notes about what they heard.

Closing (5 minutes)

Tell the group that session 2 has no starred entry point because completing a gifts inventory will be the Exploring the Word activity for that session. Stress that all need to be present to complete an inventory since their spiritual gifts will be the subject for discussion in later sessions.

Invite the music leader to lead the group in a song.

Ask if there are special concerns that group members want to pray about now and in the coming week. Then pray this prayer or one of your own, mentioning the group's concerns at the end:

Holy Spirit, as you filled and changed the disciples at Pentecost, fill us now. May your power activate in us the gifts we have been given, that the world may be filled with God's light shining through us. We ask for your love to work in us and in our world, especially on behalf of _(mention concerns named)_. Amen.

Extinguish the candle and say: **Go into the world remembering that God has no hands but ours to reach out to a hurting world, no eyes but ours to look with compassion on those who hurt. Go out to be the hands, the ears, the eyes of God this week.**

Preparing for Session 2

- Do the daily readings and entry-point activities in session 2 of the participant's workbook.

- Review the Exploring the Word activity until you feel ready to lead it.

- Review the pattern for leading *lectio divina;* photocopy and mark the week's passage for the alternate reader.

- Prepare materials for worship center, or remind the designated volunteer to do so.

- Choose an appropriate song for opening and closing the session, or remind the person who volunteered for this responsibility.

- Be sure you understand the instructions for completing and scoring the Spiritual Gifts Inventory. You will be guiding participants through this process.

- Prepare newsprint or computer presentation of words to body prayer in the Closing.

There's Only

One You

Opening prayer (5 minutes)

Light the Christ candle, saying, **Christ, we welcome you and give thanks that you are with us.** Invite the music leader to help the group sing a song.

Ask those present to think of something that makes them unique. After a couple minutes, ask each person to tell the group this unique characteristic; model by saying your sentence first. Invite the group to respond after each person speaks, **We thank you, O God, that we are fearfully and wonderfully made.**

Pray this prayer or one of your own to end the prayer time:

God of endless variety, we praise you for bringing together this group of unusual and unique—even weird—people to learn about our spiritual gifts and explore how they may be used in the name of Christ. Amen.

Interacting with the Word (15 minutes)

Divide the group into threes. Begin by allowing a couple minutes for people to review their responses to the daily readings.

Below are several questions the smaller groups (triads) might use when discussing each session's Bible reading and responses. Choose two of the questions—and others you may choose to add—for the discussion this week and gauge the group's response to them. You may use the same questions each session or vary them. Write the questions you'll be using on a board or flip chart.

Encourage group members to listen for God in each person's words. Remind everyone to allow each group member time to respond to a question before the group moves on to the next.

- What scripture passage from the past week do you remember as especially meaningful, and why?
- Which daily exercise did you most enjoy, and which was the most difficult for you?
- How did the daily readings connect to what has been going on in your life this week? Was one especially appropriate? If so, in what way?
- Which exercise surprised you or helped you realize something about yourself?
- How did the daily readings cause you to change some behavior?
- What do you want to remember from this week's readings, and why?

Exploring the Word (20 minutes)

This activity builds on Romans 12:3-8.

Ask participants to turn to the Spiritual Gifts Inventory Statements on pages 85–92 of the participant's workbook and the score sheet on page 93. The inventory is self-scoring, but caution people to wait for instructions about how to score their responses. You may need to assist group members in tallying responses. If some participants do not complete the inventory within the time allowed, ask them to complete it and score it before coming to the next meeting. (For your reference, the Inventory Key, Definitions, and related scripture are found in this book on pages 49–55).

Read these instructions for completing the survey to participants: **Read each statement to yourself twice. Respond as quickly as you can, without thinking too much, using the 7-to-1 scoring scale. Once you have completed the entire survey, add up your responses in each** horizontal line of the score sheet. Enter the total in the column at the end of the row. Circle your top score (or scores, if there is a tie); it points to your primary gift. Put a check mark beside the next three highest scores; these identify secondary, or complementary, gifts.

Give participants time to complete the inventory, then explain how to name the gifts and learn what they mean: **Using the Inventory Key (page 92 of your participant's workbook), match the numbered boxes in that far right column with names of the gifts. The Definitions on pages 94–96 of the participant's workbook describe each gift.**

Engaging the Word (lectio divina, 45 minutes)

Ask for a volunteer to read on the third hearing and direct participants to sit in groups of three.

Use the steps outlined for leading group *lectio* to guide the group through contemplation of **2 Corinthians 9:6-8,10.**

After *lectio divina*, ask for one or two minutes of silence to allow those who wish to make notes about what they heard.

Closing (5 minutes)

Invite the group members to stand in a circle to pray the following body prayer. Post an enlarged copy of the prayer in the room or display it using a computer projection system. Begin by leading the prayer responsively, asking the group to pray each line after you with the motions. The second time, invite the group members to pray with you simultaneously, using the motions. The third time, you will invite them to do the motions silently.

Placing both hands on the head, pray aloud:
God be in my head and in my understanding.

Placing both hands on the eyes, pray aloud:
God be in my eyes and in my seeing.

Placing both hands over the ears, pray aloud:
God be in my ears and in my hearing.

Placing both hands on the mouth, pray aloud:
God be in my mouth and in my speaking. *(continued on next page)*

Placing both hands over the heart, pray aloud:
God be in my heart and in my feeling.

Placing both hands on top of the thighs, pray aloud:
God be in my legs and in my moving.

Placing both hands in front of the body, one on top of the other, pray aloud:
God be in my hands and in my doing.

Raising both arms above the body, palms upward, as a sign of offering the whole self to God, pray aloud: **God be in my life and in my journeying.**

Extinguish the candle and say, **We go in peace to be the body of Christ, for that is who we are.**

Preparing for Session 3

- Do the daily readings and entry-point activities in the participant's workbook.

- Review the Exploring the Word activity until you feel ready to lead it.

- Review the pattern for leading *lectio divina;* photocopy and mark the session's passage for the alternate reader.

- Prepare materials for worship center or remind the volunteer.

- Choose an appropriate song for opening and closing the session or remind the volunteer leader.

- Assemble materials: photocopies of Spiritual Gifts Clusters and Scripture Translations to hand out (pages 54–58); list of questions in Interacting with the Word (page 32); poster or computer presentation of Buechner quotation in Exploring the Word.

Beyond the List of

"Ordinary" Gifts

Opening (5 minutes)

Light the Christ candle, reminding the group that Christ is a part of our conversation. Ask the music leader to lead the group in a song.

Then pray this prayer or one of your own:

Holy One, we are on a journey of discovery in this group. May our eyes be opened to both the ordinary and the extraordinary gifts you given each one of us. Amen.

Interacting with the Word (15 minutes)

Invite group members to sit in groups of two or three persons. Allow a couple minutes for them to review their responses to the daily readings.

Following are several questions the smaller groups (triads) might use when discussing each week's Bible reading and responses. Choose two of the questions—and others you may choose to add—for the discussion this week and gauge the group's response to them. You may use the same questions each week or vary them. Write the questions you'll be using on a board or flip chart.

Encourage group members to listen for God in each person's words. Remind everyone to allow each group member time to respond to a question before the group moves on to the next.

- What scripture passage from the past week do you remember as especially meaningful, and why?

- Which daily exercise did you most enjoy, and which was the most difficult for you?

- How did the daily readings connect to what has been going on in your life this week? Was one especially appropriate? If so, in what way?

- Which exercise surprised you or helped you realize something about yourself?

- How did the daily readings cause you to change some behavior?

- What do you want to remember from this week's readings, and why?

Exploring the Word (20 minutes)

This activity builds on 1 Samuel 16:14-23.

This will be a discussion about spiritual gifts; the inventory that participants completed last week will no doubt raise questions.

Display Frederick Buechner's words from *Wishful Thinking: A Seeker's ABC* (in the definition of *vocation*): God's call is found "where your deep gladness and the world's deep hunger meet."

Ask participants to turn to descriptions of the spiritual gifts on pages 94–96 in the participant's workbook. Distribute handout of related scripture (pages 54–55, leader's guide).

In order to see how or if the gifts of your group cluster, circulate one copy of the Spiritual Gifts Cluster list (pages 57–58) along with a colored marker or pencil. Ask each group member to anonymously place a mark alongside his or her top four spiritual gifts. (You may want to indicate your own gifts on the list before you circulate it, to offer the first few people greater anonymity.) Remind the group that no one is required to reveal their gifts. If some choose not to mark their gifts, that is fine.

After all who wish have indicated their gifts, tell the group which gifts have the most marks alongside them and which have the fewest. Invite group members to comment. Then move to a general discussion.

Here are questions to spur discussion:

- Does our group seem to lean heavily toward the private gifts or the public ones?
- What ministries might our congregation lean toward if the gifts of our group were the only ones represented?
- Do you think the lists in the scripture passages are meant to be exhaustive (are these the only spiritual gifts?), or are they meant to suggest the kinds of activities that people are gifted in?
- Is being a musician a spiritual gift? If so, why do you say so? If not, why not?
- What special and important abilities necessary for a healthy congregation do not appear in the lists from scripture?

Since scripture does not give clear descriptions of the gifts or state that there are a limited number of gifts, we have great latitude for discussion. Remind group members that no one in the early church wrote job descriptions. Anyone who reads the Bible has all the "official" information on the gifts.

Close the discussion by mentioning other resources (such as *Equipped for Every Good Work: Building a Gifts-Based Church* [Discipleship Resources, 2001]) that group members might consult if they wish to read more about the gifts.

Engaging the Word (lectio divina, 45 minutes)

Ask for a volunteer to read on the third hearing and direct participants to sit in groups of three.

Use the steps outlined for leading group *lectio* to guide the group through contemplation of **Acts 1:4-8**.

After *lectio divina*, ask for one or two minutes of silence to allow those who wish to make notes about what they heard.

Closing (5 minutes)

Extinguish the candle and say:

Go forth into the world, looking for that place where your deep gladness and the world's deep hunger meet!

Preparing for Session 4

- Do the daily readings and entry-point activities in the participant's workbook.

- Review the Exploring the Word activity until you feel prepared to lead it. Find a reference map of Paul's missionary journeys to display as part of the Exploring the Word activity.

- Review the pattern for leading *lectio divina;* photocopy and mark the week's passage for the alternate reader.

- Prepare materials for worship center, or remind the volunteer leader.

- Choose an appropriate song to sing at opening and closing of session, or remind the volunteer leader.

- Assemble materials: the list of questions in Interacting with the Word (page 36), large paper for maps in Exploring the Word, pens, pencils, markers, map of Paul's journeys.

Till All Come
to Maturity

Opening (5 minutes)

Light the Christ candle and remind the group that the candle signals that Christ is present in every conversation among believers. Ask group members to think of a time in their lives when they felt fully alive. After a minute of silence, invite them to tell the group, if they wish, what they were doing or what the setting was that made them feel completely alive. Then pray this prayer or one of your own:

> **Lord Jesus Christ, in this time together, shine your light on us. Open our eyes to see your goodness in one another. May we hear your message to us in our words to one another. Amen.**

Invite the music person to lead the group in a song.

Interacting with the Word (15 minutes)

Invite group members to sit in groups of two or three persons. Allow a couple minutes for them to review their responses to the daily entry-point exercises.

Below are several questions the smaller groups (triads) might use when discussing each session's Bible reading and responses. Choose two of the questions—and others you may choose to add—for the discussion this week and gauge the group's response to them. You may use the same questions each week or vary them. Write the questions you'll be using on a board or flip chart.

Encourage group members to listen for God in each person's words. Remind everyone to allow each group member time to respond to a question before the group moves on to the next.

- What scripture passage from the past week do you remember as especially meaningful, and why?
- Which daily exercise did you most enjoy, and which was the most difficult for you?
- How did the daily readings connect to what has been going on in your life this week? Was one especially appropriate? If so, in what way?
- Which exercise surprised you or helped you realize something about yourself?
- How did the daily readings cause you to change some behavior?
- What do you want to remember from this week's readings, and why?

Exploring the Word (20 minutes)

This activity builds on Galatians 1:13-17.

Distribute paper and pens/pencils/markers and explain that everyone will be creating a map of his or her spiritual journey. Ask people to reflect on these questions as they think about what to put on their map:

- In what place or terrain does your journey with Christ begin? Where and when did you consciously begin cooperating with what God was doing in your life?
- Show map of Paul's journeys. Have you, like Paul, spent time alone learning about God? When have you gone "into the wilderness" on your journey? How long did you stay each time? Have you spent time in different church communities? gone on mission trips?

- What individuals and groups have you learned from during your faith journey?
- Where or in what kind of place are you in now—a foreign country? a desert? a lush garden? a fallow field? a meadow filled with wildflowers? a mountaintop? at sea? Where has your journey brought you today?

Give participants time to sketch their map. Suggest that they use colored lines (like those that mark Paul's journeys) to indicate movement among the places on their map, starting with the initiation of their faith journey and ending where they are today. They may have visited some places more than once.

Invite everyone who wishes to display her or his map in the room.

Engaging the Word (lectio divina, 45 minutes)

Ask for a volunteer to read on the third hearing and direct participants to sit in groups of three.

Use the steps outlined for leading group *lectio* to guide the group through contemplation of **1 Corinthians 2:9-13**.

After *lectio divina*, ask for one or two minutes of silence to allow those who wish to make notes about what they heard.

Closing (5 minutes)

Invite the music leader to help the group sing a song.

Form a circle and ask, **What new idea do you take with you from this session?**

Pray this prayer or one of your own:

> **Lord God, giver of every good and perfect gift, we give thanks for those who are able to bake a pie, repair a car, organize an office, sing a song, comfort someone in pain, and do other ordinary tasks as part of serving you. Help us to use all of our various everyday skills to do your will. Help us to claim and use every ability the Holy Spirit energizes within us. Amen.**

Extinguish the candle and say: **Go in peace, knowing that every good gift in life is given so we can bring glory to God.**

Preparing for Session 5

- Do the daily readings and entry-point activities in the participant's workbook.

- Review the Exploring the Word activity until you feel ready to lead it.

- Review the pattern for leading *lectio divina;* photocopy and mark the week's passage for the alternate reader.

- Prepare materials for worship center or remind the volunteer who prepares it.

- Choose an appropriate song for opening and closing the session or remind the volunteer leader.

- Assemble materials: a ball of multicolored yarn, the list of questions in Interacting with the Word (page 40), copies of the questions under Exploring the Word (pages 40–41).

With a Little Help from

my Friends

Opening (5 minutes)

Light the Christ candle. Invite group members to think of a time when they have experienced what psychologists call "flow," when they became so engrossed in an enjoyable activity that time seemed to fall away. Ask them to consider whether there is a link between this activity and their primary gifts. After a minute or so of silence, invite group members to give thanks for activities that energize and renew them.

Then pray this prayer or one of your own:

> **God of joy, thank you for all the ways you renew us. Thank you for giving gifts to your people that energize us and enable us to glimpse the fullness of life that you will for each of us. Thank you for the gifts represented by those gathered here. May we encourage one another to live as your giving and gifted people, for the good of the world you love so much. Amen.**

Interacting with the Word (15 minutes)

Invite group members to sit in groups of two or three persons. Allow a couple minutes for them to review their responses to the daily entry-point exercises.

Below are several questions the smaller groups (triads) might use when discussing each session's Bible reading and responses. Choose two of the questions—and others you may choose to add—for the discussion this week and gauge the group's response to them. You may use the same questions each week or vary them. Write the questions you'll be using on a board or flip chart.

Encourage group members to listen for God in each person's words. Remind everyone to allow each group member time to respond to a question before the group moves on to the next.

- What scripture passage from the past week do you remember as especially meaningful, and why?
- Which daily exercise did you most enjoy, and which was the most difficult for you?
- How did the daily readings connect to what has been going on in your life this week? Was one especially appropriate? If so, in what way?
- Which exercise surprised you or helped you realize something about yourself?
- How did the daily readings cause you to change some behavior?
- What do you want to remember from this week's readings, and why?

Exploring the Word (20 minutes)

This will be a time to allow group members to interview one another in pairs about their spiritual gifts and then to pray for one another. Allow eight minutes for people to interview and to be interviewed, and then invite them to pray for one another. Here are questions you may duplicate or post for people to use:

- Were you surprised about any of your gifts?
- Which of your spiritual gifts had you identified or thought you might have before we completed the inventory? What caused you to think that you had this gift or these gifts?
- What have you done for or with other people that fits with your gifts as they were identified by the inventory?

- Do you understand more about activities you've tried but felt frustrated about after identifying your spiritual gifts?

- Do you feel reluctant to use any of your gifts? If so, why?

- What new ventures are you considering as a result of learning more about your spiritual gifts?

After the interviews, direct the group members to ask, "What do you want me to pray for as you think about using your spiritual gifts?" Give them a minute each to talk about this, and invite everyone to pray. They may pray silently or aloud. If they choose to pray silently, ask them to say "Amen" to end their prayer. Ask everyone to be silent when they finish, since others may still be praying. When you see that everyone has finished praying, move to *lectio divina*.

Engaging the Word (lectio divina, 45 minutes)

Luke 1:39-43, 46-48

Ask for a volunteer to read on the third hearing and direct participants to sit in groups of three.

Use the steps outlined for leading group *lectio* to guide the group through contemplation of Luke 1:39-43, 46-48. After *lectio divina*, ask for one or two minutes of silence to allow those who wish to make notes about what they heard.

Closing (5 minutes)

Have participants form a circle at least ten feet in diameter. Direct them to move until persons are about three feet apart. Holding the ball of yarn, invite group members to think about the spiritual gifts listed in the Bible passages you've been exploring. Tell them that you are going to name a gift, and, while holding on to the end of the yarn, toss the rest of the ball to someone in the circle. That person will name a spiritual gift, hold on to the strand of yarn, and toss the ball to someone else. This will continue until all of the gifts are named. The result of the activity will be a multicolored web of yarn that connects everyone in the circle to everyone else. Ask the group what this says to them about spiritual gifts.

Ask the music leader to help the group sing.

Invite group members to take part in the closing prayer by each offering a one-sentence prayer. Tell the group you will close the prayer. Ask if there are special concerns for prayer in the coming week. After these are mentioned, say, **Let us pray . . .** and wait for people to voice their prayers. Close the prayer by giving thanks for all the gifts represented by the people in your circle, ending with: **Use us, O God, to show your love as we respond to the needs around us. We ask your special care for** _(name concerns)_ **. . . Amen.**

Extinguish the candle and say: **Go into the coming week reassured that you are not alone, that you are linked to God's people by a bond that cannot be broken.**

Preparing for Session 6

- Do the daily readings and entry-point activities in the participant's workbook.

- Review the Exploring the Word activity until you feel comfortable leading it.

- Review the pattern for leading _lectio divina;_ photocopy and mark the week's passage for the alternate reader.

- Prepare materials for worship center, or remind the volunteer who does this.

- Choose an appropriate song for opening and closing the session, or remind the volunteer leader.

- Assemble materials: a small, empty gift-wrapped box for each participant, the list of questions in Interacting with the Word (page 44).

Not Hearers

Only

Opening (5 minutes)

Light the Christ candle. Invite group members to think of a time when they have felt drawn or "called" to something they did not want to do. How did they respond? After a moment of silence, say, **We'll be encountering Moses today, a man who was hesitant to follow God's call.** Pray this prayer or one of your own:

O God, when presented with the evidence of our giftedness, help us to listen for your guidance and to respond with willingness to use those gifts in your service. Amen.

Interacting with the Word (15 minutes)

Invite group members to sit in groups of two or three persons. Allow a couple minutes for them to review their responses to the daily entry-point exercises.

Below are several questions the smaller groups (triads) might use when discussing each week's Bible reading and responses. Choose two of the questions—and others you may choose to add—for the discussion this week and gauge the group's response to them. You may use the same questions each week or vary them. Write the questions you'll be using on a board or flip chart.

Encourage group members to listen for God in each person's words. Remind everyone to allow each group member time to respond to a question before the group moves on to the next.

- What scripture passage from the past week do you remember as especially meaningful, and why?

- Which daily exercise did you most enjoy, and which was the most difficult for you?

- How did the daily readings connect to what has been going on in your life this week? Was one especially appropriate? If so, in what way?

- Which exercise surprised you or helped you realize something about yourself?

- How did the daily readings cause you to change some behavior?

- What do you want to remember from this week's readings, and why?

Exploring the Word (20 minutes)

This activity builds on Exodus 3:4, 7, 10-11; 4:1-2. It is a guided meditation based on Moses' encounter with the burning bush and his attempts to avoid God's call. Pause at each ellipsis to allow group members to respond to the suggestion. Prepare to lead this meditation by doing it yourself so that you can judge how long to make the pauses.

Before you begin, invite the participants to get comfortable. Introduce the meditation by saying something like this: **This will be a guided meditation. There is no right or wrong way to do this, and whatever you experience (including falling asleep, if that happens to you) is okay. Closing your eyes probably will help you to block out distractions. Some people have trouble seeing images when they are suggested. If that's you, don't worry about it or try to force yourself to experience something. Just think about the words and ideas as they are suggested. This meditation is based on the story of God calling to Moses out of the burning bush and Moses' responses. I will read a few verses from Exodus 3 and Exodus 4, and then I will ask you to let yourself begin to imagine as I speak. Remember, there is no right or wrong way to do this. Let's begin.**

(Remember to read slowly and pause long enough to let images form in people's minds and then a while longer to allow them to explore emotions or associations that may arise within them.)

Please listen to these words from scripture:

"When the LORD saw that [Moses] had turned aside to see, God called to him out of the bush. . . . The LORD said, 'I have observed the misery of my people who are in Egypt. . . . So come, I will send you to Pharaoh to bring my people the Israelites out of Egypt.' But Moses said to God, 'Who am I that I should go to Pharaoh? . . . Suppose they do not believe me or listen to me. . . .' The LORD said to him, 'What is that in your hand?'"

Let yourself be there in the desert. . . . Feel the heat radiating up from the sand beneath your feet. . . . Feel the sun on your face, your shoulders. . . . See the strange bush—it seems to be aflame. . . . You go closer, curious, . . . and you see that the bush is on fire. . . . You watch, and you see that the bush is not being burned. . . . You wonder what this could mean, . . . and then you hear God's voice—amazing, powerful but somehow not frightening. . . . It is a voice that, somewhere deep within yourself, you realize that you already know. . . . God says to you, "I will send you. . . . I will send you."

And suddenly, you decide that this isn't right . . . that you cannot be the one. . . . Let yourself become aware of the thoughts and feelings swirling inside of you. . . . Finally, you find your voice and you say, "But who am I? Why would you send me?" . . . Let yourself become aware of resistance beginning to rise inside of you. . . . What holds you back? . . . Do you think that you don't have the time to do what God asks, that life is just so busy? . . . that you are not smart enough? . . . that you don't have the influence? . . . that you don't have enough education? . . . that you don't have the skills? . . . that you won't know what to say? . . . that you don't have the money? . . . the energy? . . . You want to say yes, but the idea seems overwhelming. . . .

God speaks again, this time asking, "What is that in your hand?". . . You look down, and you wonder what God means. What you have seems so ordinary to you. . . . YOU seem so ordinary. . . . But then God says, "What you already have in your hand—who you already are—that is enough." . . . This seems impossible. . . .

Imagine God saying to you, "What about all the things you can do? . . . What about the things that have always come easily to you? . . . What about the things you love to spend time on? . . . You have to admit that there are some things you can do well. . . . But they don't seem like holy things; they're just things you do every day. . . . Still, God asks, "Will you use those things as I ask you to?" . . . *[longer pause here]*

Imagine God saying to you, "What about your experiences? They're part of what you have in your hand." . . . Think about Moses. He grew up in Pharaoh's court; he got a good education. . . . What about the opportunities you have had? . . . What about living where you did? What did that teach you? . . .What about your very first job? What did you learn? . . . What about other jobs you've had? . . . Think about your family. Did they teach you who you wanted to be, or show you who you didn't want to be? . . . Picture the places you've traveled to. . . . Think about the training you've had, long ago. . . . Think about your childhood friends . . . and those you've had as an adult. . . . Remember the times when you have sat with someone you cared about during a painful time. . . . Think about the groups you have been a part of. . . . Think about the losses you have known . . . even the painful things you've been through—when you were a child, . . . when you were a young adult, . . . perhaps even now. . . . What about the happiest time of your life? . . . What about the times when you've felt good about yourself for doing what needed to be done, even though it was tough? . . . Listen as God asks, "What is that in your hand? Will you offer me your experiences?" . . . *[longer pause here]*

But as you look inside yourself, is there still some reluctance? even fear? . . . Still God asks, "What is that in your hand?" . . . Can you offer your feelings of inadequacy? . . . Can you offer what you know you cannot do? . . . Listen as God whispers, "Just as I was with Moses, I will be with you. You are not alone. . . . Let me use what is in your hand. Will you offer it to me?" . . .

Allow God to sit with you. . . . Feel God's love for you . . . God's reassurance. . . . Now leave the desert and the sun and come back here. . . . When you are ready, open your eyes. . . .

Allow a minute for people to stretch. Ask if anyone wants time to write in a journal. If so, request a few minutes of silence before moving on to the *lectio divina* portion of the session.

Engaging the Word (lectio divina, 45 minutes)

Ask for a volunteer to read on the third hearing and direct participants to sit in groups of three.

Use the steps outlined for leading group *lectio* to guide the group through contemplation of Romans 12:1-3.

After *lectio divina*, ask for one or two minutes of silence to allow those who wish to make notes about what they heard.

Closing (5 minutes)

Stand in a circle. Invite all to be silent and to look back over the group's meetings. Ask them to recall one gift they have received from your time together. After a minute or so, invite any who wish to name aloud a gift they want to remember. Distribute the small gift boxes, saying, **Put your box where you will see it often, to help you remember that God wants to reach out to the world through you.**

To close, use the body prayer again. Display a copy of the prayer in the room and remind the group of the motions as you pray the corresponding lines. Then invite the group members to pray with you, using the motions. Then do the motions silently.

Placing both hands on the head, pray aloud:
God be in my head and in my understanding.

Placing both hands on the eyes, pray aloud:
God be in my eyes and in my seeing.

Placing both hands over the ears, pray aloud:
God be in my ears and in my hearing.

Placing both hands on the mouth, pray aloud:
God be in my mouth and in my speaking.

Placing both hands over the heart, pray aloud:
God be in my heart and in my feeling.

Placing both hands on top of the thighs, pray aloud:
God be in my legs and in my moving.

Placing both hands in front of the body, one on top of the other, pray aloud:
God be in my hands and in my doing.

Placing both arms at the sides of the body, palms upward, as a sign of offering the whole self to God, raise the arms and pray aloud:
God be in my life and in my journeying.

Extinguish the candle and say: **Go in peace, remembering always that you are God's gifted people.**

Inventory Key, Definitions, Scripture

Inventory Key

1. Wisdom	11. Compassion
2. Knowledge	12. Healing
3. Administration	13. Discernment
4. Apostleship	14. Teaching
5. Shepherding	15. Helping/Assistance
6. Faith	16. Evangelism
7. Miracles	17. Servanthood
8. Prophecy	18. Exhortation
9. Leadership	19. Tongues
10. Giving	20. Interpretation of Tongues

Definitions

Administration—the gift of organizing human and material resources for the work of Christ, including the ability to plan and work with people to delegate responsibilities, track progress, and evaluate the effectiveness of procedures. Administrators attend to details, communicate effectively, and take as much pleasure in working behind the scenes as they do in standing in the spotlight.

Apostleship—the gift of spreading the gospel of Jesus Christ to other cultures and to foreign lands. Apostleship is the missionary zeal that moves us from the familiar into uncharted territory to share the good news. Apostles embrace opportunities to learn foreign languages, visit other cultures, and go to places where people have not had the opportunity to hear the Christian message . The United States of America is fast becoming a mission field of many languages and cultures. It is no longer necessary to cross an ocean to enter the mission field. Even across generations, we may find that we need to "speak other languages" just to communicate.

Compassion—the gift of exceptional empathy with those in need that moves us to action. More than just concern, compassion demands that we share the suffering of others in order to connect the gospel truth with other realities of life. Compassion moves us beyond our comfort zones to offer practical, tangible aid to all God's children, regardless of the worthiness of the recipients or the response we receive for our service.

Discernment—the ability to separate truth from erroneous teachings and to rely on spiritual intuition to know what God is calling us to do. Discernment allows us to focus on what is truly important and to ignore that which deflects us from faithful obedience to God. Discernment aids us in knowing whom to listen to and whom to avoid.

Evangelism—the ability to share the gospel of Jesus Christ with those who have not heard it before or with those who have not yet made a decision for Christ. This gift is manifested in both one-on-one situations and in group settings, both large and small. Evangelism is an intimate relationship with another person or persons that requires the sharing of personal faith experience and a call for a response of faith to God.

Exhortation—the gift of exceptional encouragement. Exhorters see the silver lining in every cloud, offer deep and inspiring hope to the fellowship, and look for and commend the best in everyone. Exhorters empower others to feel good about themselves and to feel hopeful for the future. Exhorters are not concerned by appearances; they hold fast to what they know to be true and right and good.

Faith—the exceptional ability to hold fast to the truth of God in Jesus Christ in spite of pressures, problems, and obstacles to faithfulness. More than just belief, faith is a gift that empowers an individual or a group to hold fast to its identity in Christ in the face of any challenge. The gift of faith enables believers to rise above pressures and problems that might otherwise cripple them. Faith is characterized by an unshakable trust in God to deliver on God's promises, no matter what. The gift of faith inspires those who might be tempted to give up to hold on.

Giving—the gift of the ability to manage money to the honor and glory of God. Beyond the regular response of gratitude to God that all believers make, those with the gift of giving can discern the best ways to put money to work, can understand the validity and practicality of appeals for funds, and can guide others in the most faithful methods for managing their financial concerns.

Healing—the gift of conducting God's healing powers into the lives of God's people. Physical, emotional, spiritual, and psychological healing are all ways that healers manifest this gift. Healers are prayerful, and they help people understand that healing is in the hands of God. Often their task is to bring about such understanding more than it is to erase negative symptoms. Some of the most powerful healers display heartbreaking afflictions themselves.

Helping—the gift of making sure that everything is ready for the work of Christ to occur. Helpers assist others to accomplish the work of God. These unsung heroes work behind the scenes and attend to details that others would rather not be bothered with. Helpers function faithfully, regardless of the credit or attention they receive. Helpers provide the framework upon which the ministry of the body of Christ is built.

Interpretation of Tongues (see also Tongues)—the gift of (1) the ability to interpret foreign languages without the necessity of formal study in order to communicate with those who have not heard the Christian message or who seek to understand, or (2) the ability to interpret the gift of tongues as a secret prayer language that communicates with God at a deep spiritual level. Both understandings of the gift of interpretation of tongues are communal in nature: the first extends the good news into the world; the second strengthens the faith within the fellowship.

Knowledge—the gift of knowing the truth through faithful study of scripture and the human situation. Knowledge provides the information necessary for the transformation of the world and the formation of the body of Christ. Those possessing the gift of knowledge challenge the fellowship to improve itself through study, reading of scripture, discussion, and prayer.

Leadership—the gift of orchestrating the gifts and resources of others to accomplish the work of God. Leaders move people toward a God-given vision of service, and they enable others to use their gifts to the best of their abilities. Leaders are capable of creating synergy, whereby a group achieves much more than its individual members could achieve on their own.

Miracles—the gift of an ability to operate at a spiritual level that recognizes the miraculous work of God in the world. Miracle workers invoke God 's power to accomplish that which appears impossible or impractical by worldly standards. Miracle workers remind us of the extraordinary nature of the ordinary world, thereby increasing faithfulness and trust in God. Miracle workers pray for God to work in the lives of others, and they feel no sense of surprise when their prayers are answered.

Prophecy—the gift of speaking the word of God clearly and faithfully. Prophets allow God to speak through them to communicate the message that people most need to hear. While often unpopular, prophets are able to say what needs to be said because of the spiritual empowerment they receive. Prophets do not foretell the future, but they proclaim God's future by revealing God's perspective on our current reality.

Servanthood—the gift of serving the spiritual and material needs of other people. Servants understand their role in the body of Christ to be that of giving comfort and aid to all who are in need. Servants look to the needs of others rather than focusing on their own needs. To serve is to put faith into action; it is to treat others as if they were Jesus Christ. The gift of service extends our Christian love into the world.

Shepherding—the gift of guidance. Shepherds nurture others in the Christian faith and provide a mentoring relationship to those who are new to the faith. Displaying an unusual spiritual maturity, shepherds share from their experience and learning to facilitate the spiritual growth and development of others. Shepherds take individuals under their care and walk with them on their spiritual journeys. Many shepherds provide spiritual direction and guidance to a wide variety of believers.

Teaching—the gift of bringing scriptural and spiritual truths to others. More than just teaching Christian education classes, teachers witness to the truth of Jesus Christ in a variety of ways, and they help others to understand the complex realities of the Christian faith. Teachers are revealers. They shine the light of understanding into the darkness of doubt and ignorance. They open people to new truths, and they challenge people to be more in the future than they have been in the past.

Tongues (see also **Interpretation of Tongues**)—the gift of (1) the ability to communicate the gospel to other people in a foreign language without the benefit of having studied said language (see Acts 2:4) or (2) the ability to speak to God in a secret, unknown prayer language that can only be understood by a person possessing the gift of interpretation. The ability to speak in the language of another culture makes the gift of tongues valuable for spreading the gospel throughout the world, while the gift of speaking a secret prayer language offers the opportunity to build faithfulness within a community of faith.

Wisdom—the gift of translating life experience into spiritual truth and of seeing the application of scriptural truth to daily living. The wise in our faith communities offer balance and understanding that transcend reason. Wisdom applies a God-given common sense to our understanding of God 's will. Wisdom helps us remain focused on the important work of God, and it enables newer, less mature Christians to benefit from those who have been blessed by God to share deep truths.

Scripture Translations

The categories of gifts are derived from Paul's listings of spiritual gifts in Romans 12:6-8; 1 Corinthians 12:4-11, 27-31; and Ephesians 4:11. The following contemporary translations from the Greek are by Dan R. Dick.

Romans 12:6-8

Each of us is gifted in unique ways, to the measure of grace given us by God; the gift of prophecy (speaking God's word) in proportion to one's faithfulness; the gift of servanthood, in service; the teacher, in teaching; the one who encourages, in encouragement; the giver, in generous stewardship ; the leader, in diligence; the compassionate, in sacrificial kindness.

Gifts listed:
1. Prophecy
2. Servanthood
3. Teaching
4. Exhortation (Encouragement)
5. Giving
6. Leadership
7. Compassion

1 Corinthians 12:4-11

There are many different gifts, but they all emerge from one Spirit; and there are many different ways to serve, but one Lord that we all serve; there are many things we can do, but it is God who directs us to do them. Everyone has been given a spiritual gift to use for the common good. To one person the Spirit gives wisdom, and to someone else knowledge by the exact same Spirit. Another receives the gift of faith, while the same Spirit grants gifts of healing to another. To others the Spirit grants the gift of miracle working, or prophecy, or the discernment of spirits, or speaking in other tongues, or interpreting other tongues. All of these gifts are activated by the same Spirit, who grants gifts to each person as the Spirit chooses.

Additional gifts listed:
8. Wisdom
9. Knowledge
10. Faith

11. Healing
12. Miracles
13. Discernment
14. Tongues
15. Interpretation of Tongues

1 Corinthians 12:27-31

Now you are the body of Christ, and each one of you is a member in it. God has appointed in the church first apostles, second prophets, then teachers, miracle workers, healers, helpers, administrators, and those who communicate in foreign tongues. Is everyone an apostle? Are all people prophets? teachers? miracles workers? Does everyone heal or speak in foreign tongues, or interpret those tongues? While it is right and good to pursue such gifts, I will show you an even more excellent goal.

Additional gifts listed:
16. Apostleship
17. Helping/Assistance
18. Administration

Ephesians 4:11-12

The gifts that the Lord gave are these: apostleship, prophecy, evangelism, shepherding, and teaching so that everyone might equip the saints for ministry, to build up the body of Christ.

Additional gifts listed:
19. Evangelism
20. Shepherding

Spiritual Gifts

Clusters

Nurturing Gifts: Nurturing congregations tend to be very committed to building fellowship, visitation, small groups, Sunday school, and member care. The focus is primarily turned inward.

- Wisdom
- Shepherding
- Exhortation
- Helping
- Discernment
- Faith
- Compassion

Outreaching Gifts: Outreaching congregations tend to be very missional in nature, serving the community in a variety of ways and reaching out to people in the area. The focus is on the world.

- Apostleship
- Evangelism

- Working Miracles
- Compassion
- Healing
- Servanthood
- Prophecy

Witnessing Gifts: Witnessing congregations tend to emphasize worship, Christian education, and church growth. Faith sharing is central to the life of the fellowship. The focus is local.

- Knowledge
- Faith
- Prophecy
- Teaching
- Evangelism
- Exhortation
- Healing

Organizing Gifts: Organizing congregations tend to be highly structured, very organized, and program-rich. Committees and work teams involve large numbers of people. The focus is on the institution.

- Knowledge
- Administration
- Giving
- Leadership
- Helping
- Teaching
- Wisdom

(*Note:* In the work with congregations between 1986 and 2001, Tongues and Interpretation of Tongues did not appear frequently enough to emerge in a cluster pattern. Most likely, Tongues and Interpretation of Tongues would align with Outreaching and/or Witnessing clusters.—Dan R. Dick, Spiritual Gifts Inventory developer)

What Is Spiritual Formation?

HUMAN BEINGS ARE creatures of the future. Unlike other inhabitants of creation whose lives are fixed within the boundaries of genetics and instinct, human existence is open-ended, laced with mystery, like moist clay in a potter's hand. We are works in progress, shaped by the constant rhythms of nature and the unexpected turns of history. Sometimes elated and sometimes burdened by our unfinished condition, we live our days conscious that "what we will be has not yet been made known" (1 John 3:2). A sense of our true identity is always just beyond our grasp, always awaiting us, it seems, just around the next bend in the road.

As nature and history interact with a human existence that is incomplete, pliable, and rich with significant potential, personal formation occurs. ***Human beings are formed by the sculpting of will, intellect, and emotion into a distinct way of being in the world.*** Such formation of personal character will assume a wide range of expression depending on our location geographically, socially, economically, and culturally. Family values, social conventions, cultural assumptions, the great turning points of an epoch, the painful secrets of a heart—these and many other factors combine to form or deform the direction, depth, and boundaries of our lives. Formation is therefore a fundamental characteristic of human life. It is happening whether or not we are aware of it, and its effect may as often inhibit as promote the development of healthy, fulfilled humanity.

For people of biblical faith, nature and history of themselves are not the final sources of personal formation. Rather, they are means through which the God who formed all things molds human beings into the contours of their truest destiny: the unfettered praise of God (see Isa. 43:21). To be shaped by God's gracious design is a particular expression of personal formation—spiritual formation. Irenaeus, third-century bishop of Lyons, echoed this ancient biblical theme when he observed that *"the glory of God is the human being fully alive."* The God known in scripture is a God who continuously forms something out of nothing—earth and heaven, creatures great and small, a people who call upon God's name, the "inmost being" (Ps. 139:13) of every human life. Yet the majestic sweep of God's formational activity never eclipses the intimacy God desires and seeks with us. Having carefully and lovingly formed each of us in the womb, God knows us by name and will not forget us (see Isa. 43:1; 44:21, 24). In the biblical perspective, to be a person means to exist in a relationship of ongoing spiritual formation with the God whose interest in us extends to the very roots of our being.

For Christians, the pattern and fulfillment of God's work of spiritual formation converge in a single figure—Jesus Christ. Jesus is the human being fully alive, fully open to God's work in the world. Simultaneously, Jesus is God's work fully alive, fully embodied in the world. For all who are heavily burdened and wearied by the torments of the world, for all who long to dwell in the house of the Lord, Jesus is the level way, the whole truth, and the radiant life. Christians are placed daily before the greatest of all choices: *to be conformed to the luminous image of Jesus Christ* through the gracious assistance of God the Holy Spirit or to be conformed to the ravaged image of the world through the deceitful encouragement of the "cosmic powers of this present darkness" (Eph. 6:12).

Spiritual formation in the Christian tradition, then, is a lifelong process through which our new humanity, hidden with Jesus Christ in God, becomes ever more visible and effective through the leading of the Holy Spirit. *Spiritual formation at its best has been understood to be at once fully divine and fully human—that is, initiated by God and manifest in both vital communities of faith and in the lives of individual disciples.* We see this theme carried through the history of the church, from Paul's introduction of formation in Jesus Christ as the central work of Christian life (Gal. 4:19) to early formational writings such as the Didache (second century); to the formative intent of monastic rules; to the shaping purpose of Protestant manuals of piety; to the affirmation of lay formation in the documents of Vatican II; and finally to the current search for practices that open us to God.

OUR NEW HUMANITY

Our unfinished character leads us to acknowledge that *"what we will be has not yet been revealed."* Yet Christians, looking at Jesus Christ, can add with confident hope that "we will be like him" (1 John 3:2). This hope originates in the hidden dimensions of baptism. Baptism unites us with the full sweep of Jesus' life and death, resurrection, and ascension in glory to the eternal communion of love enjoyed by our triune God. In baptism, motifs of cleansing from the stain of sin coexist with images of death and rebirth to signal the radically new life we enter through this spiritual birth canal (John 3:1-6).

At the center of this rebirth from above is the Paschal mystery—*the pattern of self-relinquishment and loving availability Jesus freely manifested in his ministry and in his final journey* to Jerusalem and Golgotha. This is the mysterious pattern of God's work in the world, the pattern of loss that brings gain, willing sacrifice that yields abundance, self-forgetfulness that creates a space for the remembering God. It is the pattern that steers our course from bondage to freedom—from the ways of the old Adam, who turned and hid from the One who so lovingly formed him, *to the freedom of the new Adam*, Jesus Christ, who lives with God in unbroken intimacy.

This unfolding of baptismal grace in daily life, this passing from bondage to freedom, is spiritual formation. Because *spiritual formation draws us into the fullness of life in Jesus Christ*, it shares the qualities of Jesus Christ. Thus, spiritual formation is eminently personal yet inherently corporate: *It erases nothing of our unique humanity but transposes it into a larger reality*—the mystical body of Jesus Christ in and through which we are, as the Episcopal Book of Common Prayer notes, "very members incorporate" of one another. Spiritual formation is also fully human, reflecting our own decisions, commitments, disciplines, and actions. At the same time, *spiritual formation is wholly divine, an activity initiated by God and completed by God*, in which we have been generously embraced for the sake of the world.

THE HOLY SPIRIT'S LEADING

The sweeping movement of grace by which the world was created and is sustained is orchestrated by God the Holy Spirit. In God's sovereign freedom, the Holy Spirit stirs where the Spirit chooses. Remarkably, *the Spirit has selected human life as a privileged place of redemptive activity.* In the day-to-day rhythms of our life, the Holy Spirit comes to us with gentle persistence, inviting us to join the wondrous dance of life with God. In this holy dance the Spirit always takes the lead, a partner both sensitive and sure. *"The spiritual life is the life of God's Spirit in us,"* notes spiritual writer Marjorie Thompson, "the living interaction between our spirit and the Holy Spirit through which we mature into the full stature of Christ and become more surrendered to the work of the Spirit within and around us."

There are settings and disciplines that prepare us to recognize and respond to the Holy Spirit's invitation. The church, the body of Jesus Christ visible and tangible in the world, as rich with promise as it is with paradox—is the principal context in which to sharpen our spiritual senses. The mere fact of gathering with others on the Lord's Day reminds us that the Holy Spirit continuously draws together what evil strives to scatter. In congregational worship, we hear God's word to us; recall how lavishly God loves us; see this love enacted in baptism; taste its sweetness and its wonder in the Lord's Supper; and take stock of our response to it in confession, hymn, and corporate prayer. Small groups given to prayer, study, or outreach also offer places to increase our awareness of the Holy Spirit's leading. In the company of faithful seekers, another person's moment of vulnerability, a truth spoken in love, or a story told in trust can awaken insight into ways the Holy Spirit is also present with us. Family life, which Martin Luther placed ahead of the monastery as the true school of charity, provides many opportunities to learn the art of self-forgetfulness. *Time spent with the poor and needy instructs us in our own poverty*, prepares us to receive more than we bestow from those who often seem so distressingly different, and gives the Spirit occasion to teach us the extent of our common humanity.

Personal spiritual practices also prime us to be responsive to the Holy Spirit's approach. The meditative reading of scripture encouraged in this Meeting God in Scripture series enables us to become at home in God's Word. As this occurs, we develop a growing familiarity with the Holy Spirit who fashioned and continues to dwell in holy writ. According to twelfth-century Cistercian abbot Peter of Celle, such reading is nothing less than "the soul's food, light, lamp, refuge, consolation, and the spice of every spiritual savor." *Prayer, that royal road to deepening intimacy with God, will inevitably acquaint us with the guiding grace of the Spirit.* It is in the Spirit that we pray and through the Spirit that the inarticulate yearnings of our heart receive coherent expression before God (see Romans 8:27). Various "spiritual fitness" exercises, including abstaining from self-destructive activities and attitudes, allocating personal resources in a godly manner, and following simple rules of life help to **remind us that God is the center of each day**. Such exercises produce stamina for continued acceptance of the Holy Spirit's invitation to "come and follow."

Following the leading of the Holy Spirit builds in us a growing capacity for extraordinary witness to God's kingdom, such as extending forgiveness where there has been genuine injury. It also reinforces in us the knowledge that **our new humanity in Jesus Christ is the work of the Spirit and not our own achievement.** In our human weakness, we need the strength and sustenance of the Holy Spirit to maintain the Godward direction of our life. Such assistance is clearly promised by Jesus: "When the Spirit of truth comes, he will guide you into all the truth" (John 16:13). This truth is what the author of Ephesians calls "the full stature of Christ" (Ephesians 4:13). The measure of this truth is nothing other than love. **Love is the first gift of the Spirit and the final test of our freedom in Jesus Christ** (see 1 Corinthians 13; Galatians 5:22; Colossians 1:8). All other marks of our new humanity—joy, peace, patience, kindness, generosity, faithfulness, self-control—are manifestations of this love, a love that binds us to Jesus Christ in the unity of the Holy Spirit for the sake of the world God loves so much. "If we live by the Spirit, let us also be guided by the Spirit" (Galatians 5:25).

IN THE WORLD

In a life increasingly given to the guidance of the Holy Spirit, our new humanity in Jesus Christ gradually becomes more visible and effective in the world. Far from removing us from the messiness of the world, **spiritual formation plunges us into the middle of the world's rage and suffering.** It was to this place of pain and bewilderment that Jesus Christ was sent as the visible image of the invisible God (see John 14:9; Colossians 1:15). It was to this place of bitterness and infirmity that Jesus Christ was sent, not to condemn but to save (see John 3:17). Those who are being formed in his image take the same path. Love, the full measure of Christian maturity, impels us with kindly urgency in this direction. **Love desires to be seen, known and received, for by these actions it grows wider and deeper.** Through us love is extended to the furthest recesses of human sorrow and need. Thus, God's love for the world—in us because we are in Jesus Christ—becomes a sign of hope and a source of transformation in the world.

"No one is richer, no one more powerful, no one more free," observed Thomas à Kempis, "than **the person who can give his whole life to God and freely serve others with deep** *humility and love.*" To embody in thought, word, and deed the love of God made known in our Lord Jesus Christ is the signal mark of faithful discipleship, the inexhaustible strength of vital congregations, and the ultimate goal of spiritual formation.

—*John Mogabgab*

Moving Forward in

Spiritual Formation

IN HIS ARTICLE "What Is Spiritual Formation?" John Mogabgab defines spiritual formation as "a lifelong process through which our new humanity, 'hidden with Jesus Christ in God,' becomes ever more visible and effective through the leading of the Holy Spirit." Evangelist E. Stanley Jones said, "We are Christians under construction." Thinking of our spiritual life as a process, as a journey, helps us to continually make progress toward the goal of being conformed to the image of Jesus Christ.

First, we journey forward in faith. The Christian life is lived in relationship with Jesus Christ. We express our faith in Jesus through the character and conduct that emerge from that relationship. Our "belief system" is the total expression of who we are and what we do. The ongoing process of spiritual formation begins and continues with faith. Having given ourselves to God through an initial commitment, we subsequently respond to God, so that our faith grows deeper and stronger. The Holy Spirit is the dynamic energy conforming us to the likeness of Christ in personal and social holiness.

We never "graduate" from the spiritual life. Instead, we awaken each day to discovery. Frank Laubach began each day by praying, "God, what are you doing in the world today that I can help you with?" We move forward in spiritual formation believing that God does indeed invite us into holy partnership.

Second, we move forward with a sense of "fit." When David volunteered to fight Goliath, King Saul clothed him with the royal armor (see 1 Sam. 17:38). Because the armor didn't fit, David gave it back to Saul, preferring his own clothing and his own weaponry—five stones and a slingshot. David's strategy may have been contrary to all standards of military preparedness, but it worked! Likewise, our approach to God in spiritual formation must "fit" each of us individually. The Christian life is a way of the heart, and we must follow our hearts in the way we move forward in spiritual formation. Spiritual formation is not random or subjective, however. On the contrary, the choices we make will conform to the larger patterns of faith development in our lives.

As you read the scriptures, you will undoubtedly find that certain approaches will be more valuable and meaningful than others. They may seem more comfortable. Go forward in the directions that have benefited you most. Don't worry about what you are *not* selecting; concentrate on the tradition or path that produces righteousness, peace, and joy in your life (see Rom. 14:17).

Along the way, you may find yourself circling back to a previous method or expanding into new areas. Just as with clothing so also with the soul; there will come those times when you "outgrow" the methods you are using and feel the need to develop in new and different ways. Remember that outgrowing something does not mean leaving it behind. It merely means increasing the size. You will inevitably arrive at such turning points in your spiritual life. When the time is ripe for change, you will know it. For now, work with the principles and practices that best fuel your desire for deeper life in God.

A sense of "fit" also means tailoring your spiritual practices to the realities of your life. What are you experiencing now? Develop a devotional life that takes your circumstances into consideration. In fact, you will not continue to move forward if you deny your needs and emotions. When these change, you can alter your practices to fit a new circumstance or emotion. God knows what you are going through. Don't be afraid to follow wherever God might be leading you on your spiritual formation journey.

Third, we move forward in the presence of friends. Spiritual formation does not happen in isolation. One sign of our genuine progress is the desire to be in "communion with the saints"—in community with others. Community is the context in which much authentic spiritual formation takes place.

Through community we express our faith in Jesus Christ—a faith that includes the conviction that Jesus has many brothers and sisters whom we are called to love and with whom we are called to live. Our faith community consists of our particular affiliation with a congregation and the related smaller groups that exist within it, as well as our spiritual friends, mentors, and teachers. Living in community educates, guides, protects, restores, inspires, forgives, heals, and sustains us and sends us out into the world.

Community is also the laboratory in which we learn what it means to be compassionate, not only to fellow Christians but also to people located throughout the world; our community extends to our wider ecumenical and mission associations with Christians around the globe.

The saints are not only those with whom we live in ongoing fellowship—they are those of renown from the past. Being in community with others means developing a devotional life that includes reading and reflecting on the classics of Christian spirituality. When we read the classics we connect with those who have gone before us. Far from being outdated or irrelevant, the classic writers are part of the great "cloud of witnesses" (see Heb. 12:1) who both inform us and encourage us in our journey.

We are blessed to have many of the spiritual classics in print today. The Paulist Press series *Classics of Western Spirituality* is one of the most extensive offerings in this regard. Upper Room Books has produced a series of short collections titled *Upper Room Spiritual Classics*. You can also find individual classics in print. Works like Augustine's *Confessions* or Julian of Norwich's *Revelations of Divine Love* are but two of hundreds of such works available for your enrichment. Anthologies are another effective way to connect with the classics. John Baillie's *A Diary of Readings* is one of the best known, containing one-page readings for every day of the year. Woodeene Koenig-Bricker's volume *365 Saints* summarizes the thoughts and contributions of well-known and little-known Christians.

Finally, we move forward by adopting a form. Faith and form are inseparable. Form provides the concrete structure on which spiritual formation is built. We are offered a variety of forms and styles, plans and programs to shape and sustain our discipleship. As we become rooted in the spiritual life, we will likely gravitate toward particular resources and practices that suit us and satisfy our needs. Our choices are determined by factors such as gender, race, personality, faith tradition, age, and stage in life. There is nothing wrong with settling into a particular form of spiritual formation. It is as normal as our choices in areas such as literature, art, and music. We never have to apologize for finding and developing those patterns to which we are drawn.

God is gracious to provide many avenues for spiritual development. A particular Bible version may provide the means to enter into the scriptures in a personal way. Or you may find a daily-office format like The Book of Common Prayer or *A Guide to Prayer for All God's People* helpful. You may enjoy feeding for an extended period of time on the writings of a single author, such as Henri Nouwen, Oswald Chambers, or Evelyn Underhill.

Though it's perfectly acceptable to choose a form that suits us, we also need to be open to broadening our experience by trying new forms, traditions, writers, and so on. There is indeed a great variety in the ways God speaks to us. A look back through church history reveals that the saints were not only deeply spiritual people but also people with broad interests that expanded and informed their spiritual formation. Catherine of Siena was involved in the political affairs of her day. John Wesley was fascinated with medicine. Peter Marshall was a great game player.

There is a world of blessing and benefit available to us when we embrace all the experiences God offers us. If our spiritual formation is grounded in the Bible, we stand on a sure foundation that enables us to reach upward and outward to every dimension of development that God—who created the earth in all its fullness—has provided.

As you enter into the process offered in this Meeting God in Scripture series, you will not only encounter Holy Scripture directly but also encounter the elements that enable you to move forward in spiritual formation: faith, fit, friends, and form. These are the roadmaps that will guide your journey—a journey that none of us can plan or control.

The earliest Christian creed contained only three words: "Jesus is Lord!" It was the simplest way believers knew to declare their utter confidence in the risen Christ to lead and guide them into an abundant and everlasting life. Wherever you are right now, there is good news: God loves you more than you can imagine. Move forward with assurance. The best is yet to be!

—*J. Steven Harper*

Meeting God in

Service

TEN CHAIRS WERE pulled close together in a circle, but we were all leaning forward to catch Mary Jean's words. She seldom spoke during our small-group meetings, yet this week she seemed eager to talk. She described the time she had spent working in a community center and the relentless problems of poverty, addiction, and abuse she had encountered there. Tears came to her eyes as she concluded, "I feel helpless as I look at these families and see their suffering. What does God expect of me? How can I make a difference?"

Like Mary Jean, *we may struggle to see just how God acts in a world of great suffering.* And when it comes to our own role, we often don't know where to begin or what God might be asking of us. We sometimes feel overwhelmed, and we want to turn away from the realities that surround us. Yet as we begin to serve others, we often find our hesitations fading. *We discover that when we help others we encounter God. We meet God in the midst of our efforts.* This can happen in several ways.

LEARNING TO LOOK

We learn to see God by opening our eyes and actively looking for opportunities to serve others. From the beginning of his ministry, *Jesus constantly stayed alert to people and their needs.* It was one reason why he came. Jesus read from the book of Isaiah in the synagogue at Nazareth, applying these words to himself:

"The Spirit of the Lord is upon me,
>   because he has anointed me
>   to bring good news to the poor.
> He has sent me to proclaim release to the captives
>   and recovery of sight for the blind,
> to let the oppressed go free,
>   to proclaim the year of the Lord's favor."—Luke 4:18-19

Every day as he traveled with his disciples Jesus healed and fed and loved people. A number of stories in the Gospels tell us that *Jesus acted because he was moved with compassion.* As painful as it must have been, *he did not turn aside from people's suffering.*

Jesus not only saw the sufferings of human beings but also became involved in people's suffering to heal and bring new life. The story of the widow of Nain in Luke 7:11-17 illustrates this. As Jesus travels with his disciples and a crowd of followers, he encounters a funeral procession. The widow, he discovers, has lost her only son. Jesus sees her grief with eyes of compassion, knowing that as a widow she has been completely dependent on her son. Now she has no one—and nothing. Jesus says to her, "Do not weep," and raises the young man back to life. Then we find the words, "Jesus gave him to his mother" (v. 15). What compassion and mercy are captured in those words!

Again and again Jesus actively seeks the sick and needy. He goes directly to them; he notices their pain and suffering and responds with divine grace and love. *The common activities of his life—travels, conversations, seemingly chance meetings with people—become the settings for expressions of his caring alertness.* He appropriately perceives himself as a servant of God, and in serving God he ministers to those God loves.

LEARNING TO LISTEN

In the Gospel of John, Jesus demonstrates that this open-eyed attitude of caring was not to be confined only to his own ministry but was to characterize his followers' lives as well. *Jesus washed the disciples' feet as they gathered to celebrate the feast of the Passover, in part to remind us of our proper posture before others*: "You call me Teacher and Lord—and you are right, for that is what I am. So if I, your Lord and Teacher, have washed your feet, you also ought to wash one another's feet" (John 13:13-14). Not only do we open our eyes to need; we also listen to those we serve. We cannot know how to help others if we simply barge in to "fix" a list of problems we think we see in them. *We are to serve others with gentle openness and with a willingness to relinquish our own agenda.* We listen to their ideas and hopes and longings.

To listen requires a quieting of our own interests and experiences so that we can become open not only in that particular relationship but also to the ways in which God is present in the relationship. Henri J. M. Nouwen writes, "Real training for service asks for a hard and often painful process of self-emptying. The main problem of service is to be the way without being 'in the way.'"

Learning to become more open to others teaches us many things. *Openness cultivates in us an attitude of honesty.* We see ourselves, as well as others, more clearly. Then we are able to open ourselves to God—to let the Great Healer have those parts of us that are wounded and in need of healing and forgiveness. Just as we speak of God's love for and forgiveness of others, so we can claim that healing in our own lives.

Our lives may be deeply changed as we serve others. *As those we serve share their own pilgrimages, we see how God has been a part of their experiences.* Their vision of God may enlarge ours. Their words, feelings and desires may challenge us in surprising ways. When twentieth-century spiritual writer Evelyn Underhill went to Baron von Hügel for guidance about her relationship with God, he recommended that she spend a designated amount of time each week directly serving the poor so as to break open her heart to the needs of people and open her up more fully to experience God's grace. As a result she met a woman named Laura Rose, the beginning of a relationship that was to become deeply significant for Underhill's spiritual growth.

LEARNING TO LOVE

To looking and listening we add loving—of the most radical, sacrificial kind. It is easy to be captured by our own special interests and by self-absorption. *When we follow Jesus, however, normal priorities get turned upside down.* We confront what German pastor and theologian Dietrich Bonhoeffer called "the cost of discipleship."

God thereby transforms our self-interest into a new awareness of our interdependence. We identify the ways in which we need one another in order to grow in faithfulness. We find a new identity by centering our lives in the One who is the light of the world and who calls us to let our lights "shine before others, that they may see your good works and give glory to [our] Father in heaven" (Matt. 5:16). We realize that nothing matters more than bringing people to Jesus for healing and salvation.

Little by little our hearts, which can so easily become hardened to the needs of others, are changed into caring and compassionate hearts. Thomas Kelly, in his book, *A Testament of Devotion*, captures this phenomenon in these words: "God plucks the world out of our hearts, loosening the chains of attachment. And . . . hurls the world into our hearts, where we and [God] together carry it in infinitely tender love."

RESOURCES TO GET US THROUGH

The radical call to service does not pose for us an impossible duty, however. ***God promises to give us the power and resources we need*** through the indwelling spirit of Jesus. Paul wrote to the new converts in the first-century church in Corinth to remind them of their calling. Paul pointed out that he had come to them in weakness, fear and trembling, but that God had used him to demonstrate the power of the Spirit (see 1 Cor. 1:18-31; 2:6-13). What freedom there is in knowing that God can use us in spite of our weaknesses!

Indeed, power is released through our vulnerability. ***It is through our vulnerabilities that we learn the nature of God's sufficiency.*** The only way we can confront head-on the pain of a suffering world is through utter reliance on God's grace. We can take to heart God's word to Paul, "My grace is sufficient for you, for power is made perfect in weakness" (2 Cor. 12:9).

Jesus is inviting us to love the world as he loves. Paul encouraged a congregation of Christians who were undergoing much struggle by reminding them that they were a letter of Christ, written not with ink but with the Spirit of the living God (2 Cor. 3:2-3). What a word of promise for today! ***We go in the power of the Spirit.*** The Spirit speaks in and through what we do.

"Christian ministry," writes James Fenhagen, "is more than doing good. Ministry is an act of service performed either consciously or unconsciously in the name of Christ. Ministry is Jesus Christ expressing his life through us." ***When we are tempted to run and hide because the needs of the world are overwhelming and we feel helpless to make a difference, we can remember that we do not go alone.*** We venture out boldly, not because we underestimate or devalue the needs and woundedness of others but because we trust in the steadfast and abiding love of God.

In serving the needs of others in society, we meet God. We find joy, as Brother Lawrence found centuries ago, "doing little things for the love of God." And as we grow, we learn more about the love of Jesus and what it means to share it with others. This prayer in Ephesians describes what it means to mature in our relationship with Jesus: "I pray that, according to the riches of his glory, [God] may grant that you may be strengthened in your inner being with power through his Spirit, and that Christ may dwell in your hearts through faith, as you are being rooted and grounded in love" (Eph. 3:16-17).

—*Janice T. Grana*

Meeting God in

Community

WE WERE NOT CREATED to live in isolation. No person "is an island, entire of itself," wrote the poet John Donne. While no one questions the need for periods of solitude and refreshment in our lives, faith tends to thrive most readily when shared with others. *Without the connections community affords us, we experience what someone once called "spiritual loneliness."* For we meet God not just as we sit alone in quiet corners but in and through the people with whom we live, work, and interact as we go through our daily routine.

Relationships present us with both a remarkable privilege and an awesome responsibility. Proverbs 27:17 tells us that "iron sharpens iron, and one person sharpens [and shapes] the wits of another." *As other people's lives touch ours, they help to form our faith and make us who we are.* As we touch others, we reflect God's love to them.

Relationships with other believers have extraordinary power in our lives because Jesus is present in them. *Jesus knew the importance of people in conveying God's grace and presence.* "Where two or three are gathered in my name," he said, "I am there among them" (Matt. 18:20). Within our churches, small groups, families, and friendships, we learn from one another. We find encouragement. We challenge one another to follow God more faithfully. Other Christians enable us to walk as we should when we might otherwise have strayed or wandered. ***God uses relationships to form us, and relationships form us so that God can use us.***

The Bible offers many examples of the formational power of relationships. The story of Ruth and Naomi demonstrates how ***the presence of other believers can enable us to do what we can't do alone.*** Ruth is a foreigner, a Moabite who has married Naomi's son. When Naomi's husband and her sons (including Ruth's husband) die, she grieves, saying, "The hand of the LORD has turned against me!" (Ruth 1:13). Ruth, also widowed, chooses to stay with Naomi rather than return to her own kin. Ruth speaks the words that are well-known and much-loved: "Where you go I will go; where you lodge, I will lodge; your people shall be my people, and your God my God" (Ruth 1:16). Just think of the magnitude of the change those words brought about! Something in this relationship makes Ruth willing to leave her family and country to adopt Naomi's faith. The younger woman seeks guidance from Naomi and in turn cares for her. Their loving relationship releases Naomi from the bitterness of her losses and draws Ruth into relationship with the God of Israel. Eventually Ruth becomes the ancestor of Jesus the Messiah (see Matth. 1:5).

Elijah and Elisha offer an example of the way God uses the power of relationships to build strong leaders. ***God, employing Elijah as Elisha's mentor, makes a dramatic difference in the life of the younger man who is eager to serve God faithfully.*** Elijah, a famous prophet, is near the end of his ministry when God tells him to seek out and anoint Elisha as his successor. Elijah throws his cloak over Elisha's shoulders as the younger man walks behind his plow and oxen, publicly calling Elisha to a new way of life. What a dramatic act! Elisha leaves his farm work to become Elijah's attendant (see 1 Kings 19:16-21), following the prophet and seeking to learn from him. He refuses to leave his mentor and asks for "a double portion" of the spirit that has made Elijah great (see 2 Kings 2:9). One man is clearly the teacher and the other the student, and, like Elijah, ***Elisha acknowledges that God is at the center of his life and ministry.*** Through his relationship with Elijah, he develops the courage, faith, and skills to carry on the work of the prophet as God's spokesman.

In the New Testament Mary and Elizabeth offer us yet another example of how relationships help us mature in faith. ***Their relationship illustrates the value of sharing*** *mutual insight and encouragement.* According to the Gospel of Luke, young Mary is visited by the angel Gabriel, who tells her that she will bear a son who will be the Messiah. Mary, "much perplexed by his words" (Luke 1:29), hurries to visit her older cousin Elizabeth, who is also pregnant. Though Mary has told the angel that she wants to be obedient to God's will, she is surely also confused and frightened. But after Elizabeth speaks to her, Mary breaks into a song of praise to God; her faith has been strengthened. Mary spends three months with Elizabeth, who supports her and in turn is supported in the joyful yet sacrificial work to which God has called both of them. Mary discovered, as many have, that *when we are hesitant to face what lies ahead, spending time with someone who knows us and shares our faith can help us see more clearly* and understand more deeply the issues we need to deal with. It fortifies us to move forward in faith.

SOUL FRIENDS

Throughout the history of the church, writers and leaders have echoed this message. In the twelfth century, Aelred of Rievaulx said that *Christian friendship can be "a step to raise us to the love and knowledge of God."* He also spoke of the joy of having a friend with "whom you need have no fear to confess your failings; one to whom you can unblushingly make known what progress you have made in the spiritual life; one to whom you can entrust all the secrets of your heart and before whom you can place all your plans." Teresa of Avila wrote in the sixteenth century of how *"it is a great advantage for us to be able to consult someone who knows us, so that we may learn to know ourselves."* John Wesley went so far as to declare that there is no such thing as a solitary Christian.

What these Christians from various times and places learned is that *God uses close and continuing relationships to form us into the image of Jesus.* As we share both our high moments and our low, pray for one another, help each other, and work together toward common goals, we reflect Jesus and acknowledge Jesus' presence with us.

NURTURING YOUR OWN SOUL FRIENDS

To begin to meet God in community you may want to reach out to other believers with whom you can discuss your spiritual journey. Such conversation helps you sort out what you know about yourself and about God. It may be especially valuable if this action is deliberate. Ask one or two mature individuals with whom you can exchange thoughts and prayers with confidence and assurance of confidentiality to meet with you. This practice has traditionally been called "spiritual guidance," "spiritual direction," or "spiritual friendship." This kind of conversation may also occur in the context of worship services, church school classes, and small groups. One-on-one relationships and small groups allow for a depth of interaction not possible in larger, more formal settings. They allow us to pray aloud for one another with potentially life-changing results. As Alan Jones, an essayist on Christian friendship, stated, "We cannot help but tremble on the brink of surrender, but it is our companions who give us the courage to jump."

SPEND TIME OBSERVING THE LIVES OF FAITHFUL CHRISTIANS

The New Testament tells us repeatedly that *we become like Jesus by spending time with those who are his friends.* We look at those who have led us, consider the outcome of their faith and then choose to imitate them (see Heb. 13:7). Some find it a good discipline to think periodically about someone whose faith they admire. Consider approaching one or more such people to ask them how God has been at work in their lives. (For biblical examples of this process, see 1 Cor. 4:6; Phil. 3:17; 1 Thess. 1:6; and 2 Thess. 3:9.)

STAY ACTIVE IN A CHURCH COMMUNITY

As happens within our immediate family circle, when we rub shoulders with others we are continually confronted with reminders of our weaknesses and brokenness. We wound others and are wounded by them. Romans 12:18 acknowledges that living with others can be difficult, urging, "If it is possible, so far as it depends on you, live peaceably with all." While imperfections abound within what Paul calls "the body of Christ," *God still uses the company of believers to grace our lives and transform the world* (see Rom. 12:4-5; 1 Cor. 12:12; Eph. 5:30). We cannot do without our fellow believers. Let us "not [neglect] to meet together," the writer of the letter to the Hebrews urges (10:25). At their best, relationships with other believers not only shield us in difficult times but also help us to confront our imperfections. We find a place to mutually speak "the truth in love" (Eph. 4:15).

VIEW YOUR INVOLVEMENT WITH OTHER BELIEVERS AS AN OPPORTUNITY TO HELP

It is a privilege to nurture another person, to be trusted to hear another's dreams and concerns, to pray for someone. In so doing we may discover myriad ways to use the gifts that God has given us for the benefit of our family in Christ as well as for our own growth and enjoyment. As we help others, we too will be helped. As we comfort and teach and encourage, we will be comforted, taught, and encouraged in turn. As we experience community, we find our lives enriched, in turn providing us with more to give to others.

Meeting God in

Everyday Life

"WE LIVE LIVES OF LITTLE THINGS," someone once said. We are occupied most often with the details of ordinary life. Driving to the office or factory, putting supper on the table, taking feverish kids to the doctor—these are the things that fill our hours. When we meet God, that encounter often takes place in and through everyday circumstances. Growing spiritually will mean "living to God on common occasions," as Horace Bushnell expressed it. *Inevitably we cultivate our spiritual lives not just in quiet solitude but in the activity of everyday life.* We realize that God speaks to us not just in sky-rending revelations but also in the intimacy of quiet conversation with someone we love, the freshness of a child's spontaneous observation, the warmth of a bubbling pot of chili, the comfort of a familiar household ritual.

How do we meet God in the midst of our stressful, busy lives? How do we recognize the signs that, in Avery Brooke's wonderful phrase, lie "hidden in plain sight"? Two intentions will help:

REMEMBER GOD'S DEEDS

The Bible leaves no doubt that God works through the inner and outer details of our everyday lives. And if God is present in such moments, we cannot let them slide into oblivion: "Watch yourselves closely, so as neither to forget the things that your eyes have seen nor to let them slip from your mind all the days of your life" (Deut. 4:9). The psalmist, recalling God's careful involvement in Israel's history, vowed, "I will call to mind the deeds of the LORD; I will remember your wonders of old" (Ps. 77:11).

The act of remembering helped the people of Israel to keep events from the past vital in the present. Just as we pull out a photo album on a rainy day in order to recall the significant moments of our lives—to review the snapshots of graduations and baptisms, visits and vacations—so God wanted the people of Israel to keep their holy history vividly present in their minds. And they were to remember God's good deeds corporately, as a people. Recollection was a community event. As they gathered in various ways, the people recalled aloud the moments that had given them identity as people of God—when God led them to freedom from Egyptian bondage, gave them commandments and instruction, gave them life. "Remember the former things of old," Isaiah enjoined the people, speaking on God's behalf (Isa. 46:9). *The Israelites' very identity depended on the God who had acted in their history. To forget God's acts would have meant to forget that God had called and chosen them.*

God's call to remember carried over into New Testament times. Jesus urged his followers to commemorate God's work of redemption. "Do this in remembrance of me," he said at the Last Supper (Luke 22:19). Communion, in which we partake of the bread and the cup, is a supreme act of remembering. We also meet God through recalling what he has done for us personally. With David the psalmist we make certain that we "do not forget all [God's] benefits" in our daily lives (Ps. 103:2). To jog his readers' memories, David recites specific benefits. He does not indulge in nostalgia but gleans from the past what the Lord did and said. *When we remember the Lord's deeds, we likewise keep in the forefront of our minds what God has already shown us; we live in continuity with the events that have shaped us.* We recall the blessings of last year and the hardships of last week, remembering how God walked beside us and sometimes carried us in our moments of weakness and woundedness.

Conscious recollection requires discipline. In a live-for-the-moment culture, we may find the act of remembering more difficult than ancient people did. We are prone to become distracted by the details of the moment. We forget to "read life backwards." But memory can be a powerful resource for keeping our spiritual perspective alive.

One practical aid to this holy remembering is keeping a journal. Many find it helpful to jot down prayers, record insights from Bible readings, or put on paper the events that seem to be leading somewhere—events that have left an impression on them. Keeping a journal can be done in a way that meets your own needs and preferences. Journaling need not be an elaborate affair or something you slavishly do every day. It can be as simple as you wish and as occasional as meets your need. If you have never used a journal, take a blank bound book, a spiral notebook, or a binder full of paper—and simply write. Make your writing an act of sanctified listening. When you write down your thoughts and ideas and emotions, they take definition and shape. You may find that as you write, you begin to untangle your confusion about what you are hearing from God. You may hear God speaking in ways that you may not have been attentive to otherwise.

Do not allow yourself to relegate to a fuzzy memory the significant events and changes going on within and around you. "The simplest ink," says an old Chinese proverb, "is more reliable than the finest mind." Writing becomes a way to extract deeper meaning from what has happened to you. It becomes an act of remembering.

Leaf back through your journal pages every few weeks. Notice how God's purposes seem to be emerging in what has happened—and in what hasn't happened. Thank God for prayers that have been answered. Continue to lift up to God themes that emerge from what you've written, themes that reveal your heart's desires. And watch for a greater sense of personal direction. Keeping a journal, wrote Ronald Klug, is "like walking into a messy room—toys and clothes and books piled around—and slowly picking things up and putting them in their right places again. The room 'feels good' and I can go on living there. In a similar way, my journal helps me sort out things in my life and restore some internal order" (from *Keeping a Spiritual Journal*).

We can practice the art of remembering when we meet with family and friends. Conversations at family reunions might move beyond talk of sports or vacations to reflections about how God has proven faithful in our family's past and present stories. And when we go to church, worship can be an exercise in remembering. Spiritual-growth groups, church-school classes—any gathering of believers—can be an occasion to track God's actions. We recall ways God has been faithful. We "testify." When we do, we are reminded of who God is through what God has done.

REFLECT ON GOD'S DEEDS

Reflection—alert awareness of what is happening now—returns us to the present moment. *Open-eyed reflection allows us to see God's hand at work or to grasp insights we might otherwise have been too busy to notice.* The Bible sometimes uses the word *meditate* for this kind of thoughtful reflection. We are not talking about the meditation of Eastern religions nor a privatized, overly individualistic quest for religious experience. Biblical meditation is always God-centered. It often focuses on God's Word revealed in scripture. And it often has to do with God's activity. "On your wondrous works, I will meditate," David exults in Psalm 145:5. Just three verses earlier he had vowed, "Every day I will bless you." An awareness of what God is doing and the impulse to praise God go hand-in-hand.

Events of daily life therefore belong in our daily prayers. In the Lord's Prayer Jesus directs us to pray for God's will to be done on earth, not just in heaven—which means in our everyday lives. Knowing how much daily matters affect us, Jesus even encourages his followers to pray for "daily bread"—the everyday sustenance that keeps our physical bodies going. The likelihood that Jesus worked as a carpenter during his early adult years implies that God, through Jesus Christ's incarnation, has for all time graced daily work. And God notices when "bad" things happen and operates through events so that, as the apostle Paul wrote, "All things work together for good for those who love God" (Rom. 8:28). All the realities of life, then, constitute the grist for our conversations with God.

As we pray about what happens to us from moment to moment, we begin to cultivate spiritual alertness. Jean-Pierre de Caussade wrote of "the sacrament of the present moment." He meant that the place where we are, the actions that we take, can mediate God's presence. Writing of Mary and Joseph, Jesus' parents, de Caussade asks, "What do they discern beneath the seemingly everyday events which occupy them? What is seen is similar to what happens to the rest of [hu]mankind. But what is unseen, that which faith discovers and unravels, is nothing less than God fulfilling [a] mighty purpose. . . . God reveals [God]self to the humble in small things" (from *The Sacrament of the Present Moment,* translated by Kitty Muggeridge).

Reflection can take place in the workplace, where many of us spend much of our time. Martin Luther, one of the prime figures of the Protestant Reformation, argued that not just priest or nun but also milkmaid or blacksmith could become deeply conscious of God's presence. This awareness can happen in our busy times and during our leisure times. Thomas Kelly writes, "A life of little whispered words of adoration, of praise, of prayer, of worship can be breathed all through the day" (from *A Testament of Devotion*).

Staying alert to God's presence may be as simple as pausing to acknowledge that God is near. It may mean taking a few moments to pray during a lunch hour or coffee break. It may mean occasionally looking out the window to drink in the beauty of God's creation or paying care-filled attention to the people with whom we live. And it certainly means allowing everyday blessings—a sunset, a smile from a friend—to remind us of God and point us toward God in gratitude.

—*Timothy Jones*

About the Author

Mary Lou Redding's

favorite book in the world to read is the Bible, whose Old Testament characters feel like personal friends. Having read their stories so many times, she feels they have become part of her personal history because she sees herself in their struggles and acknowledges their weaknesses as her own. Her fascination with God's using such imperfect and at times unwilling people to accomplish divine purposes makes her consider that God might use even her.

Redding has a Master of Arts degree in Rhetoric and Writing and has worked professionally as a writer and editor for many years. She helped to create and contributed to *The Spiritual Formation Bible* and has published a number of books with Upper Room Books: *Breaking and Mending: Divorce and God's Grace, While We Wait: Living the Questions of Advent,* and *The Power of a Focused Heart,* a small-group study of the Beatitudes. She experiences God's grace and presence and serves within the community of faith at Brentwood United Methodist Church in Brentwood, Tennessee.

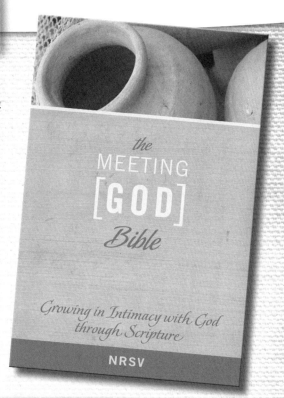